Contents

Acknowledgements

Thanks are expressed to Ken Falconer (photographs and advice), Keith Kellett and Keith Noble (photographs), Chris Butterfield, Robert Hearing, Eric Perks and Tony Youngs (artwork), Joan Whitaker of the British Walking Federation, and numerous event organisers and LDWA local group secretaries for permission to use badge, certificate and logo designs.

W...
ch...

Firs...
len...
walking...
the great majority of events...
prizes or trophies for the fastest man or woman to finish the course, and the last person home is as much a 'winner' as the first person to cross the line. The goal is to overcome the personal challenge of completing a route, usually within a fixed time scale. Much encouragement and advice is generally available from other walkers and non–walkers, and willing assistance is normally on hand, providing food and drink, first aid and transport. However, in the end the walk is completed by the individual who is determined to rise to and overcome the challenge.

Firm adherents of challenge walking believe that their sport is one of the best, as it combines three important elements: plenty of exercise, leading to fitness and health; an exploration of the countryside on foot, over all types of terrain; and camaraderie and friendship amongst people from all walks of life.

Challenge walking on the whole avoids roads and so participants generally don't suffer from many of the overuse injuries experienced by road runners constantly jarring bones and tendons on a hard surface. Moreover, the scenery of the varied countryside is far superior to that on the average urban marathon. Challenge walking appeals to young and old alike who wish to spend a day or more out in the countryside, amongst agreeable company and with a pre-planned objective.

It is extremely difficult to provide a precise, all-embracing definition of a challenge walk, as there are so many different types and variations. As the title suggests there must be a degree of challenge in such a walk, but even this is difficult to define. A serious challenge to one person may be a simple afternoon stroll to another. Most, but not all, challenge walks satisfy the following criteria:

1. they are over a fixed, stated distance, along a pre-determined route
2. for a successful completion, the route must be covered within a given timescale
3. they are not races and there is no award for the fastest times
4. some form of memento is given to all those who successfully complete the walk. This may be in the form of a certificate, cloth badge or medal.

Distance

Challenge walks have been held over distances ranging from a few miles to many hundreds of miles. However, the majority are rarely less than 10 miles (16 km) long and seldom exceed 100 miles (160 km), and within this range most challenge walks are between 20–30 miles (32–48 km) in length.

Time limits

Most, but again not all, challenge walks have quite generous time limits, allowing all but the very slowest to complete the course within the allotted time. On relatively easy, lowland terrain, time limits usually allow for a pace of $2\frac{1}{2}$–3 miles (4–5 km) per hour to complete the route. For example, a walk of 25–30 miles (40–48 km) along footpaths and bridleways in the south of England typically has a time limit of between 10–12 hours. In upland areas over moorland and mountain the time allowance is usually far more generous.

There are two reasons why most challenge walks have time limits. Firstly, it adds a little to the challenge to complete the course within a set timescale. The second reason, and perhaps the more important one, is simply for practical purposes; it would be unreasonable to expect volunteer checkpoint marshals to stay out on the course for an indefinite period waiting for those walkers who had decided to make a prolonged stop en route.

On some events there are 'cut-off points' on the course which are designed to prevent overdue walkers from struggling on in a vain attempt to finish the course within the allotted time span. For example, a 30–mile (48-km) event may have a cut-off point of '2.30 pm after 20 miles at checkpoint 5'. The checkpoint staff will have been instructed to retire all walkers who arrive at that checkpoint after that time. A 'sweeper' is often employed to ensure that all reach the event headquarters safely.

The challenge walker

Challenge walkers come from all walks of life and firm friendships are often made between people who, in the normal course of their lives, would be most unlikely to meet.

Long distance walking calls for stamina and determination rather than physical strength, and so women are just as likely as men to become good long distance walkers. Indeed, from a physiological point of view, women are possibly better equipped for long distance walking than men. Many are just as keen as their male counterparts and it is perhaps significant that several top long distance walkers are women.

Age groups

Long distance challenge walking appeals to people of all ages. The adage 'you are never too old to learn' applies to challenge walking as it does to so many other pursuits. Mental and physical stamina increases until middle age, and therefore long distance walking, unlike many other sports where participants tend to peak early in life, is not exclusively a young person's activity.

Many septuagenarians and even a few octogenarians are regular challenge walkers, some even completing the longer distance events. At least five people have completed a Hundred (*see* p. 17) when they were over 70.

Long distance walking helps to keep body weight down, lungs and heart healthy, and muscle in good tone.

Long distance walking presents a real challenge and this is probably why it appeals to the young. Many people in their early teens are regular challenge walkers, whilst a few have achieved tremendous feats of endurance at a very early age. Although challenge walking is to be encouraged in the young, some caution should be exercised to prevent possible damage to growing limbs and muscles. Participation in the longer events should be avoided until the age of 16–18 years. If in doubt, it is best to consult a doctor who has experience of long distance walking or running.

Other activities

A few people take up challenge walking without ever having participated in any other sort of walking activity or sport in the past. Most people, however, were walkers for several years before they discovered long distance challenge walking. Some are ramblers who are looking for a little more challenge in their walking from time to time. Others have walked several of the long distance footpaths or National Trails in the UK and/or abroad, and have taken up challenge walking as an additional activity. Many challenge walkers are primarily hill or mountain walkers, whilst some are seasoned backpackers. All enjoy companionship, the countryside and the thrill of completing different routes.

Yet more people enter challenge walking from an athletic background. Road or marathon runners may become tired of pounding the streets and look for another activity which enables them to get off the roads and out into the countryside. Running on hard surfaces can also lead to foot or leg injuries and some sufferers change to walking on footpaths to alleviate these problems. Runners may grow tired of the competitive element in road races, but still want something with an element of challenge. A few challenge walkers are retired race walkers who still enjoy long distance walking.

How to enter a challenge event

Sources of information

Details of challenge walking events can be found from a variety of sources: walking and outdoor magazines, local libraries, youth clubs, youth hostels, scout huts, etc. There are three particularly useful sources of information. Firstly, the monthly magazine *The Great Outdoors* publishes a 'diary' section in each issue which gives brief details of forthcoming challenge events, together with the names and addresses of event organisers from whom further details and application forms can be obtained.

Secondly, the most comprehensive listing of challenge walking events in Britain is found in *Strider*, the magazine of the Long Distance Walkers Association (LDWA). Details of the majority of walking events to be held over the following 6–8 month period are included, together with the names and addresses of event organisers. For inclusion in the 'List of events', which is compiled by the Events' Secretary of the LDWA, an event must satisfy a few simple criteria, mainly that there must be an entry limit of 500 and that, if the event is intended to raise money for a particular cause, entry to the event should not be confined to those who agree to seek sponsorship. *Strider*, published three times a year, is available only to members of the LDWA, but membership is open to all on payment of a modest annual fee.

An additional source of information is the *Events Calendar* published each year by the British Walking Federation (BWF). This contains details of all BWF (IVV) events in Britain.

Entry

Having obtained a contact address for the event, send off for further details and an entry form, not forgetting to enclose a stamped addressed envelope for the reply. After receiving further details, check to make sure that: the walk is within your capabilities, you are eligible for entry, you like the area over which the event is to take place, and you are happy with the other details of the walk. A few events have lower age limits, e.g. 16 or 18 years, whilst others insist that participants below a certain age (commonly 14 years) are accompanied by an adult. It is often a condition of entry that persons under 18 years of age will only be permitted to walk if a parent's or guardian's written consent has been obtained. Make sure that you can comply with these rules.

Fill in the details on the application form carefully before adding your signature. By so doing you will normally be agreeing to the rules of the event, including obeying the Country Code; the organisers will not be held responsible for any injury or loss which may result during or after the event. Post the application form, together with the relevant entry fee, well in advance of the date of the event. Some events have a closing date for entries, often two or more weeks before the day of the walk. It is usual to enclose an SAE if confirmation of entry is required. This is essential with some events in order to receive a set of final instructions.

Some events allow entry on the day, although often the entry fee will be somewhat higher than the fee paid in advance. If entering on the day, ensure that you arrive in plenty of time to register before the start of the event.

Preparations

Prepare a list of essential items of kit that must be carried (*see* Appendix), making sure that you own them or can buy or borrow them for the day. Ensure that you have the Ordnance Survey map of the area (these can sometimes be borrowed from public libraries). Make a note of whether refreshments are available at the checkpoints en route and at the finish. If not, then ensure that you take a plentiful supply of your own food and drink (it is recommended that some food for use in emergencies is always carried, whether or not refreshments are provided by the organiser).

Dogs

If you intend to take your dog(s) with you, be sure to read the event details carefully, or if in any doubt contact the organiser before taking your pet along. Many walks cross farm land where livestock is kept and for this reason dogs are often not allowed. Where dogs are permitted, ensure that only well trained animals are taken and that they remain with the owner on a tight leash throughout the event. It only takes one dog to cause damage to farm property or

A walker with his dog on the Brecon Beacons Hundred

threaten livestock, and so put the entire event in jeopardy, thereby losing the goodwill between walkers and landowners that so many organisers and walkers do much to foster.

Taking part in a challenge event

Let's suppose that you are taking part in your first challenge event. Although every one is a little different, with its own special atmosphere, most of them run to a familiar pattern; the following describes a typical day event and what you might expect to happen.

The venue

A description of how to get to the venue, sometimes with a grid reference of the start, will probably be given in the further details sent with the application form or in the final details despatched before the date of the event. The event will sometimes be signposted, or occasionally marshals are posted. Other marshals will probably be on duty to direct cars to the car park. Those entrants without private transport must ensure that they can reach the venue on time by public transport, or can be given a lift by another walker or friend.

Registration

On arrival at the venue, which may be a school, village hall or community or sports centre, be sure to register straight away. The registration desk will probably be divided into 'pre-entry' and 'entry on the day'. If you have already entered by post, go to the former queue and give your name and, if available, your entry number. You will be handed a set of route descriptions (if these were not sent prior to the event), probably a sketch map of the route and possibly a list of minor route amendments. You will also receive a tally card and walk number. Keep this safe and dry, as you will have to produce this for punching or stamping at all of the checkpoints en route. Listen carefully to any instructions that the entry marshal may give you and note in particular where and at what time you must assemble for the start. There may also be a kit check at this registration; it is most important that you have the necessary equipment to satisfy the kit check marshals (*see* Appendix). After these formalities, you are free until the start of the event.

A detailed map showing the route is often placed in a prominent position inside the start venue and now is the last opportunity to mark the route off onto your own map and to make a note

The organiser gives final instructions to walkers before they set off on a challenge event

of any last minute alterations to the course. (Note that when route details are made available before the event, the route should be marked up on your map and studied beforehand.) Light refreshments are often available prior to the start.

The start

The event will start in one of a number of ways. Most events simply have a mass start. There may be a short announcement by the organiser or his deputy before the walkers all move off together. The start is usually punctual but informal, although a few organisers use a gun or flag; one event is even started by the sound of hammer on anvil. Some events have two starting times for walkers, sometimes referred to as a 'walkers' start' and a 'fast walkers' start', the latter being half or one hour later than the former. This helps to alleviate any jostling that might occur when walkers of different speeds set off together.

A third alternative is the 'staggered start' where there is a flexible starting period (usually 1–2 hours) during which participants can choose when to

Participants assembling for the start of a challenge walk ('Gathering for the start', A. Youngs)

commence. This type of start avoids bunching at the beginning of the event and is particularly useful if there are a number of stiles to be negotiated in the early stages. Several walking events also allow runners or joggers to participate, although the latter will rarely constitute more than 10 per cent of the starting field. When runners are accommodated on an event, there will often be a 'runners' start', commonly 1 or 2 hours after the 'walkers' start'. Such staggered starts are a help to the organisers as they reduce the length of time that later checkpoints must be open in order to accommodate both walkers and runners.

Some organisers operate the following system at the start of the event. At registration the entrant will be given a 'start tally', usually a number on a small wooden disc. This must be handed in to a marshal as the walker leaves the venue at the start of the walk (usually it is dropped into a bucket or other receptacle) or a short distance after the start. The organiser then has a record of all those who actually commenced the walk.

On the walk

Once on the event, follow the route description and map to visit all of the checkpoints in the order given. On an average 25-mile (40-km) walk there will probably be 5 or 6 manned checkpoints. The typical checkpoint will be manned by two or more marshals who will record your walk number and clip your tally. It is your responsibility to ensure that this is done; if you don't, you will be disqualified.

Water or squash is normally available at all manned checkpoints and sometimes food will be provided. The quality and quantity of the refreshments vary considerably from event to event. It is sensible to carry some of your own food in case there is not sufficient at the checkpoints or if that provided is not to your taste.

On some events there will also be a number of unmanned checkpoints. These often consist of an orienteering-type clip attached to a stake. They must be located and your tally card punched at the appropriate place. Occasionally, an unmanned checkpoint will comprise a number or a word which must be recorded on the tally card.

If you cannot complete the walk, then you will have to retire. Unless you are injured or in serious trouble, this should always be done at a manned checkpoint. Report to the checkpoint marshal, giving your name and number and handing in your tally card. Under no circumstances should a walker retire without informing the event officials. Transport back to walk headquarters will then be arranged for you as soon as possible.

After the walk

Most challenge walks are circular in nature and at the end of the course the walker will return to the start venue. Remove all muddy footwear before going inside and present your tally card immediately to the timekeeper. Now is

Checking in a walker at a checkpoint ▶

the time to relax and enjoy the food and drink often provided at the end of the walk. Showers are sometimes available.

A certificate recording your success will be prepared for you whilst you wait and a badge of the walk may be provided or, more likely, will be on sale. At some events medals are available as souvenirs of your achievement. You will have finished your first challenge walk and will no doubt feel very pleased with yourself.

Remember that event organisers and marshals are volunteers, giving up their spare time to help and encourage you. A cheerful 'thank you' when you leave a checkpoint or the walk headquarters at the end of the day goes a long way to making them feel that it has been worthwhile.

One final but most important consideration. A few serious accidents and even fatalities have resulted when a walker, exhausted from a long distance challenge walk, has attempted to drive home after an event. This is particularly dangerous after overnight events where the walker has gone without sleep. Don't drive home if you are tired, but rest first. Stay overnight in a bed and

Completion certificate for the Windmill Way

breakfast or youth hostel if necessary, or arrange for someone to drive you home at the end of the walk.

Types of event

The day walk

There are several types of challenge walk organised by various clubs, organisations and individuals. It may all seem rather bewildering to the newcomer. However, the most popular event, and the one most frequently staged, is the long distance walk of between 20 and 30 miles (32–48 km) in length which takes place over a full day, with a time limit of 10–12 hours. This event is most suitable for the first timer. Most are held on either a Saturday or a Sunday, starting usually between 8 and 9 a.m. The majority are annual events, occurring on or around the same date every year, but a few are held every other year. Some are 'one-off' events, occurring only once as an organised event, although many of these are later available as 'anytime challenges' or are frequently walked by local clubs.

Light refreshments are generally available at the various checkpoints en route and it is becoming increasingly common for a meal to be provided for participants when they finish the walk at the end of the day. As a general rule, day challenge walks in lowland Britain tend to be 25–30 miles (40–48 km) in length, whereas those on the mountains and moorlands of northern Britain are usually 20–25 miles (32–40 km) long.

Distance

Several long distance day events now include optional shorter routes designed to cater for newcomers to long distance walking, for those unsure of tackling the longer distances, and for families and young children. Many of these shorter distance alternatives use part of the longer route and share checkpoints, and so the atmosphere of the long distance event is shared by all. Some events also stage a relatively short 'quiz walk', usually between 6 and 10 miles (10–16 km) long, which takes place on the day of the full event. These are often designed to appeal particularly to younger walkers and family groups. Entrants are supplied with a set of questions about aspects of the route, the answers to which will be found whilst on the walk. Points are normally awarded for each correct answer, the aim being to complete the route and answer all the questions correctly. They make a fine introduction to long distance walking.

There are several hundred day events held all over Britain throughout the year. There is really no particular season for challenge walking, but the calendar of events is especially full during April, May and June, and also in September and October. December is the only month of the year when there are very few events, but this is the time when many walking clubs hold their annual dinners and associated walks.

Several of the more well established day events are listed in table 1 (page 33–5). This is not intended to be an exhaustive list, but it does illustrate the variety and range of day challenge walks that are on offer. Several new events are staged each year, whilst others are sometimes not held for a year or two and some disappear from the calendar, never to reappear. Challenge walks are found in most parts of England and Wales, although there are relatively few long distance events in Scotland.

Cake, biscuits and plenty to drink at a checkpoint on the Cotswold Challenge at Coopers Hill

Newcomers to challenge walking would be well advised to choose a fairly short event, over relatively easy terrain, before progressing to the longer, harder events. A few event organisers whose walks are particularly suitable for novices encourage first-timers to enter, and such events are obviously ideal for those unsure of their capabilities. It is far better to enjoy a relatively short, easy event and so be encouraged to tackle something harder, than to suffer on a demanding route which may deter you from entering another challenge event.

Some events carry the name 'marathon' in their title, e.g. Malvern Marathon, Mortimer Forest Marathon. This does not usually imply that they are either 26.2 miles (42 km) in length, or that they are running races. The term 'marathon' is used here in its broadest sense. Most walking marathons are, in fact, longer than 26 miles.

Worcester Beacon from the North Hill checkpoint on the Malvern Marathon

Variety of events

Participating in different challenge events is a good way of exploring new areas that the walker may not have considered visiting before. Several new regions can be 'discovered' in this way, perhaps being visited on a later occasion for a more thorough, leisurely exploration. Many event organisers try to find areas where there is no footpath erosion, but where the passage of several hundred walkers will help to define footpaths that are barely visible on the ground. By attending such events one is helping to keep the footpath network open and usable.

Some events, such as the Clent Clamber over the Clent Hills in the West Midlands, the South Shropshire Circular over the Shropshire hills in the Marches and the Malvern Marathon in Worcestershire, traverse popular hill country. Several events are predominantly woodland walks: the Mortimer Forest Marathon in Shropshire and the New Forest Marathon are examples. The Gongoozler is an event held along canal towpaths; each year a different stretch of canal is used, usually in northern England.

The theme for some events is the circumnavigation of a well-known town, such as the Tunbridge Wells Circular and the Canterbury Circular, both in Kent. The fen country of Cambridgeshire is the scene of the Daffodil Dawdle and the Cambridge Lowland Hike. South-east England is represented by the Gatliff Marathon and the Tanners Marathon amongst many others.

Several events take place over or around the Pennine hills, including the Two Crosses Circular and Limestone Limp. The North York Moors, the traditional home of the challenge walk, is well represented by events including the Falcon Flyer and the Wheeldale Tandem, the latter event being for teams of two. The Lake District hosts the very scenic but strenuous Duddon Landscape Walk and also Spring in Lakeland, which follows a different route each year in the southern part of the National Park. As you can see, there is something to suit all tastes and abilities.

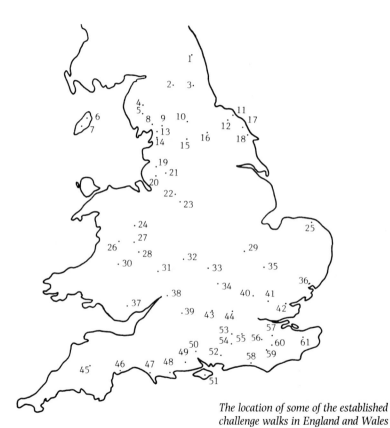

The location of some of the established
challenge walks in England and Wales

Key

1. Chevy Chase and Cheviots Challenge
2. Helm Wind Walk
3. Durham Dales Challenge
4. Spring in Lakeland
5. Duddon Landscape Walk
6. Manx Mountain Marathon
7. Castle to Castle Walk
8. That's Lyth
9. Kirby Lonsdale Walk
10. Fellsman Hike
11. Wheeldale Tandem
12. Hanging Stone Leap
13. Arnside Marathon
14. Silvarn Round
15. Ulfkil Stride
16. Kilburn Kanter
17. Smugglers Trod
18. Scarborough Rock Winter Challenge
19. Anglezarke Amble (Summer &
    Winter)
20. Wigan Pier Walk
21. Two Crosses Circuit
22. Otter High Peak Challenge
23. Leek Moors Marathon
24. Longmynd Hike
25. Poppy Line Marathon
26. Across Wales Walk
27. South Shropshire Circular
28. Mortimer Forest Marathon
29. Nene Valley Kanter

Multi–day events

There are a few events in Britain and many on the Continent which last for several days, typically four. There is usually a choice of distances to be walked on each of the days of the event. Different distances can be walked on each day if desired. There is normally a choice of accommodation available, including hotel, bed and breakfast, youth hostel and campsite. These events (*see* page 36) are renowned not only for challenging and varied walking, but also for the social atmosphere fostered by assembling several hundred challenge walkers over a number of days. There is normally a relaxed holiday atmosphere on these events and each night some form of entertainment is usually arranged.

Perhaps the most well known multi-day event in Britain is the Welsh International Four-Day Walks, which has been held every September since 1981 in Llanwrtyd Wells in Powys, mid-Wales. It runs from Tuesday until Friday in the third week of the month.

Walkers normally assemble in Llanwrtyd Wells on the Monday night for pre-event details. As well as having a different area to cover on each day of the event, there is also a choice of distances, normally 20–25 miles (32–40 km), 15 miles (24 km) and 10 miles (16 km). The long walk includes everything from minor roads to open mountainside, whilst the intermediate route is the least strenuous part of the longer walk. The short walk is on minor roads, good footpaths and forest tracks, and is led by a guide. There is something for everyone on the Welsh Four Days, being suitable for novices as well as the more experienced walker.

Of a rather different nature is the Across Ross Walk which is held annually during the first weekend in May. It offers a unique opportunity to cross northern Scotland from coast to coast in a single weekend. Walkers set out from Dingwall on the east coast on the Saturday morning to walk the 33 miles (53 km) to remote Glenuaig Lodge on the Achnashellach Estate for an overnight stop where traditional highland hospitality will be experienced. Participants walk a further 27 miles (43 km) on the following day to the village of Dornie on the west coast where, after receiving congratulations and a certificate, they may be transported back to Dingwall or Inverness. Entry is limited to 60 persons, so early application is advisable.

Kanters and orienteering-type events

The majority of challenge events are held over a fixed course which is followed with the aid of a route description issued by the organisers. However, on some events this is not provided; instead, a list of grid references is supplied. The route follows a line linking these points and makes use of rights of way and/or country which has open access.

Obviously, some skill in the use of map and compass is essential for these events. They offer an extra challenge and provide excellent practice in navigation, experience which will be extremely useful when you are on other walking activities.

Grid references

Some of these orienteering-style events have an ordered list of grid references, but in every other way are identical to the usual day event, with manned checkpoints where tally cards are checked and where refreshments are available. Other events, known as 'kanters' are primarily intended as exercises in the use of map and compass. A number of unmanned checkpoints are identified by map grid references and must be located before returning to the walk headquarters. Kanters vary in difficulty depending upon the nature of the terrain, the time allocated and the whim of the organiser(s). The number of checkpoints to be visited varies enormously from 4 or 5 to 30 or more on a day walk. On some kanters it is merely necessary to locate each unmanned checkpoint and to mark your tally card with the specific hole punch provided. Other kanters require entrants to provide one- or two-word answers to simple questions; the answers will be found at the checkpoints.

On the easier events a relatively short list of grid references will be supplied in the correct sequence, i.e. if visited in the order given, straightforward paths should be found between checkpoints, enabling the entire course to be walked by the shortest or easiest route. At more demanding events a large list of randomly arranged grid references will be supplied. The entrant is required to plot these on a map, determine the shortest and easiest route linking all the checkpoints and then return to the walk headquarters. It is advisable to spend adequate time plotting the grid references and working out your route before setting out.

On some kanters it is not always feasible to visit all the checkpoints and return to base within the allotted time. In this case it is necessary to plan a route which visits as many of the given checkpoints as possible.

Careful scrutiny of the route before setting out on a challenge walk ▶

Points kanters

On certain events known as 'points kanters', the checkpoints carry different 'weightings'. Those closer together, nearer to base or easier to find, are awarded fewer 'points' or 'marks' than those further apart, a long way from the walk headquarters or more difficult to find. The object is to amass as high a 'score' as possible within the time limit of the event. To ensure that all participants return within a reasonable time, the rules of some 'points kanters' state

that marks will be deducted for every minute after the deadline that the walker is out on the course.

Kanters appeal to those walkers wanting mental as well as physical exercise, but are beneficial to all, giving often needed practice in the art of navigation. From the organiser's point of view they are simple and cheap to stage. They can often be organised by just one person from a small village hall or even an open car park or picnic area. No marshals or checkpoint teams are required, food and drink being provided by the walkers themselves. The numerous checkpoints are usually grouped in all directions around the walk headquarters so that a walker is never too far from home and, if it is necessary to retire, he or she should be able to head straight back to base at any time. Kanters are usually between 12 and 27 miles (19–43 km) in length. Examples include the New Forest Marathon, Kilburn Kanter and several kanters organised in various parts of Surrey by the Surrey Group of the LDWA.

Ultra-long distance events

After the long distance walker has successfully completed several daytime events of between 20 and 30 miles (32–48 km), he or she may wish to tackle something a little more exacting. There are several events on the walking calendar which exceed 40 miles (64 km), most of these being classified as 'overnight' events since the walker will almost certainly have to walk through the night as well as during the day in order to complete the route within the timescale.

Entry to these ultra-long distance events is normally restricted to the walker who has some experience of long distance challenge events. Prospective entrants are usually asked to specify a challenge walk of at least 25–30 miles (40–48 km) that they have completed within the previous 12 months. The rules on such events tend to be strictly enforced for obvious reasons of safety. Failure to comply usually results in instant disqualification.

Plenty of spare, warm clothing should be taken on overnight events, as it can become very cold at night, even during the summer.

All overnight events require participants to carry torches with spare batteries and bulb. Many events, particularly those over high moorland and mountain, insist that 'grouping' takes place during the hours of darkness. In other words, walkers are allocated groups of three or more persons at the checkpoint before darkness falls. These must be maintained until daylight or until a marshal grants permission for each to split.

Practice

Walking across country in the dark, with the aid of a torch, map and compass, is perhaps not as difficult as it may seem to the uninitiated. However, it is a good idea to get some practice at night walking before embarking on an overnight event. Some of the LDWA local groups have occasional night or even overnight walks on their programmes which are led by competent night walkers, and these will provide good experience and practice in the art of night navigation. Alternatively, ask an experienced friend to accompany you on a walk at night. When out in the countryside, especially when not taking part in a night time event, it is a good idea to keep well away from houses so as not to disturb the local inhabitants or be suspected of illegal activities. For the same reasons, try to avoid areas where you might be accused of poaching.

◀ *Relaxing at a checkpoint on an overnight event*

Food and drink

Food and drink are much more important on an overnight event than they are on a day walk lasting no more than 12 hours. Event organisers usually ensure that sufficient food of a high quality and variety is available at most checkpoints. Substantial meals will also be provided at one or two checkpoints and at the end of the walk. The best advice is to eat 'little and often', rather than consume two or three large meals en route. Some walkers, like many marathon runners, practise 'carbohydrate loading' by eating an enormous pasta-style meal the night before an event.

Those who have never before undertaken an overnight event are advised to start with a relatively easy walk before attempting the more testing events. This is not always practicable since any overnight event by its very nature cannot be classed as easy. Those events in the southern half of the country generally cover gentler terrain than those in the north, but to compensate few southern overnight events are less than 62 miles (100 km) in length. Furthermore, traversing muddy paths in the south of England during the spring and autumn can be exceptionally tiring. Of the events listed in table 3 (page 37), the High Peak Marathon, for teams of four in the Dark Peak, and the Fellsman Hike in the Yorkshire Dales are exceptionally hard marathon walks and it would be advisable for a novice walker to gain some experience on other overnight events before attempting one of these.

Hundreds

Ever since the Long Distance Walkers Association was founded in the early 1970s, it has staged an annual 100-mile (160-km) challenge event. The 'Hundred', as it is affectionately known, is obviously for experienced and committed long distance walkers, but nevertheless several hundred participants are ready to test their stamina, skill and endurance every year over a tough, cross-country course.

Hundreds are nowadays organised by an LDWA local group under the auspices of the LDWA and take place in a different location each year. Over the years Hundreds have been staged in many varied and attractive areas,

including the South and North Downs, the North York Moors, Snowdonia, Dartmoor and the Brecon Beacons.

The annual Hundred always takes place over the Spring Bank Holiday weekend. The event usually commences between 10 a.m. and noon on the Saturday and has a generous time limit of 48 hours to complete the route. A stop of longer than 2 hours normally results in enforced retirement.

Requirements of entry

It is a requirement of entry that walkers are experienced and have successfully completed at least one long distance event (usually of 40 miles (64 km) or longer) within the previous 12 months. Certain items of kit, such as survival bags and torches, must be carried, and spot kit checks are made to ensure that walkers comply with the rules. (Failure to do so results in instant disqualification). A kit check list may include some or all of the following: adequate footwear (with particular reference to tread), rucksack, waterproof top and overtrousers, map with map case and compass, route description, emergency food and drink, spare, warm clothing,

torch with spare batteries and bulb, white, luminous or reflective patches for night walking, a first-aid kit, survival bag and whistle, spare laces and coins

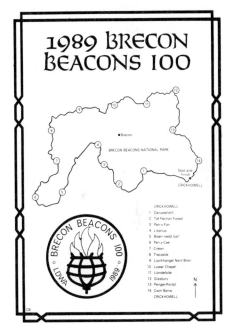

Route and badge design for the 1989 Brecon Beacons Hundred

for use in a public telephone. Several event organisers insist that personal mugs are carried and will not provide drinks in throw away cups or cartons. A check list of equipment and clothing is given in the appendix on page 40.

The appeal of Hundreds

It is no mean feat to complete a hundred-mile walk, although several thousand walkers now hold this distinction. Some walkers become addicted to the Hundred and return year after year in an attempt to gain the much respected Hundred certificate and badge. For those who have completed 10 Hundreds, there is a special, highly-prized '10 × Hundred' badge. Holders of this award are surely in the category of the 'super walker'. It requires a minimum of nine years' dedication to ultra-long distance walking.

On two previous Hundred events an opportunity was given for the really experienced walker to exceed the magical hundred mile mark. The Cumbrian Hundred in 1981 allowed walkers to continue to 124 miles (200 km) if they were capable and so desired (very few did), and the 10th Anniversary Hun-

The Downsman Hundred

Logo for the Downsman Hundred, a 100-mile challenge walk

dred in 1982 offered the chance of a 'Hundred Plus', a phenomenal 140 miles (225 km) from Winchester to Canterbury within 50 hours. Over twenty participants completed this distance.

Mountain marathons

These are two–day events usually held over a weekend. There are two well-known mountain marathons staged in Britain, the Saunders Lakeland Mountain Marathon (SLMM) and the Karrimor International Mountain Marathon.

The SLMM has been held annually since 1977, at a different location each year within the English Lake District. The event, for teams of two, is held over a weekend in mid-July with an overnight camp. Considerable expertise in mountain navigation is required. Backpacking experience is also necessary because a tent, sleeping bag, stove, fuel and food have to be carried, together with warm and waterproof clothing and emergency gear.

There are various classes covering distances between 31 and 50 miles (50–80 km) over rough mountain terrain during the two days. The main classes are the Scafell Class (Elite Standard) for top class fell runners, Bowfell Class ('A' Class Standard) for experienced navigators capable of moving quickly over steep mountainsides, and Wansfell Class ('B' Class Standard) which requires some experience of mountain walking, although no previous experience in similar events is necessary. Prizes are awarded in each class for those who complete the course in the fastest times.

The Karrimor International Mountain Marathon is held each year in October at a different venue in upland Britain. The exact location is not revealed until just before the event takes place. Previous locations have included Dartmoor, the Howgills and central Scotland. The Karrimor is similar to the Lakeland Marathon in that it is a two-day orienteering event for teams of two carrying overnight camping gear. There are three classes similar to those of the Saunders Marathon, usually covering distances ranging from 25 to 44 miles (40 to 71 km) for the two days. Like the SLMM, there is a limited entry to the various classes.

Marches

Marches were introduced to the UK from the Continent where they are extremely popular. As the name suggests, they frequently have military connections and are often organised by service units. Unlike the majority of challenge walks, most marches take place on minor roads or well defined tracks and the route is always waymarked. It is not unusual for them to attract a thousand or more walkers, many in military uniforms.

Walking in formation, particularly by military personnel, is encouraged, and banners and flags are often paraded. Medals are usually presented on completion of the route and these sometimes carry bars to denote multiple completions. Civilians are nearly always welcome on marches; they can enter either as individuals or as members of a team or club. Marches are generally between 6 and 25 miles (10 and 40 km) in length, and they rarely exceed 27 miles (43 km). The most well known marches in Britain include the Royal Military Police and City of Chichester March (held every August), the Folke-stone ATC March (May) and the British Airways International One-Day Walk in Windsor Great Park (September).

Foreign challenge walks

Challenge walking in Europe is very popular, particularly in Holland, Belgium, Denmark and Germany. Events generally tend to be along tracks and minor roads and they attract thousands of walkers. Several events are more in the nature of marches than challenge walks, most being organised by local representatives of the European IVV (*see* page 31).

The Nijmegen Marches

The most famous continental event is the Nijmegen Marches held over four days every July. The event attracts up to 25,000 participants; even the registration can take up to a whole day. The event is quite unlike any in Britain: the whole area around Nijmegen is involved in the walking and associated social activities for the duration of the Marches. It is a considerable feat accommodating and feeding such a large number of people, but the event is an important item on the tourist calendar in Holland.

The walking is mainly along roads with rather unspectacular scenery, but most participants attend for the unique, cheerful atmosphere. Participants have a choice of three distances: 19 miles (30 km), 25 miles (40 km) or 31 miles (50 km). These must be walked for four days in succession in order to qualify for a medal. Further information can be obtained from the British Walking Federation (*see* 'Useful Addresses').

The Haervejsvandring

Perhaps one of the best, albeit one of the toughest of the continental events, is the Haervejsvandring in Denmark. This is a linear walk through the country, marching 26 miles (42 km) or more each day for a period of one week. It can easily be fitted into a week's holiday, and is one of the best ways to see this low-lying north European country.

The number of participants is usually kept to a maximum of 700, walkers being accommodated in schools or army barracks each night. Medals are presented to successful walkers at the end of the event. Further information can be obtained from Marchforeningen Fodslaw St.Sct. Hansgade 9, DK – 8800 Viborg, Denmark.

The Dodentacht

The best known ultra-distance event on the continent is the 62-mile (100-km) Dodentacht or Death March, which takes place in Bornem in Belgium every August. The event attracts up to 5,000 participants from 20 countries and the walk starts on a Friday evening. Coaches are organised to take walkers from Britain to the event (for further details send an SAE to Dodentacht, 7 Northampton Road, Wellingborough, Northants NN8 3HG).

Sponsored walks

The majority of challenge walks are not organised as sponsored walks, despite the commonly held belief amongst the general public that most forms of endurance walk are designed to raise money for a particular cause. However, most organisers don't object if some participants use their event to raise money for a worthy cause. If you intend to do this, then it is advisable to check first with the event organiser and to ensure that your sponsorship campaign is a relatively low key affair.

Running and jogging

Many events which are primarily for walkers cater for a small proportion of runners or joggers. If you intend to run, then do ensure that you leave on the separate 'runners' start', if one is provided, otherwise you may arrive at checkpoints before their official opening times. You should remember that although you will be made welcome, you cannot expect, and will not receive, the sort of support provided specifically for runners on marathons or fell races. Running is not allowed on certain walking events, so don't disregard a 'no running' rule; to do so will offend walkers on the event, inconvenience the organisers and will lead to disqualification.

They're off! Walkers setting out on a typical challenge walk ▶

Equipment and kit checks

If you walk or ramble already, then it is very likely that you possess all or most of the necessary equipment. The basics for a typical day event are: suitable footwear; spare, warm clothing; a set of waterproofs (top and overtrousers); compass; and the relevant Ordnance Survey map, preferably protected in a waterproof map case. Add to this spare food and drink, and the whole can easily be carried in a small daysack.

Footwear

The type of footwear used on challenge walks is often a topic of fierce debate,

but it is probably best left to the personal preference of the walker. Boots should ideally be of the light-weight variety of which there is now a wide range of models available. Many challenge walkers prefer to wear a pair of good quality trainers, even over rough and wet ground. They argue that their lightness and comfort far outweigh the lack of ankle support and inability to exclude water. (When trainers are worn it is essential that they carry a good tread.) However, those who have always worn boots when walking in the countryside are not advised to experiment with trainers on their first challenge walk.

The majority of experienced challenge walkers wear footwear appropriate to the season and terrain. Trainers are often adequate for the dry footpaths of lowland Britain during the summer months, whilst a pair of good quality boots may be more sensible for mountain and moorland events during the winter. A few events specify that only boots with a good tread will be permissible.

For some day events, particularly those taking place on a warm, dry summer's day, a small 'bum-bag'

rather than a full rucksack may be sufficient to carry the small amount of equipment. These are often used by long distance runners and can be purchased from good sportswear shops. On a few of the longer, overnight events it is possible to have one relatively small item of baggage transported to an intermediate checkpoint. This is useful for sending on a change of clothes and footwear to be used in the later stages of the event.

Clothing

The most suitable clothing to wear while walking is largely a matter of personal choice. However, the following points are worthy of serious consideration. Never wear jeans whilst out in the countryside, particularly in upland areas. They soak up rainwater and take a very long time to dry out, exacerbating hypothermia. Breeches or walking trousers are recommended, although shorts are ideal on warm summer days.

It is better to wear a number of thin garments (e.g. thermal vest, shirt, two thin pullovers, light anorak, cagoule) which can be shed as the temperature and weather improves (the 'layer principle'), than to put on one or two bulky items.

Finally, good quality waterproofs are essential, but the newcomer would be unwise to buy expensive garments made from breathable fabrics until he or she has gained more experience and knowledge of equipment. A relatively inexpensive waterproof made from coated nylon or similar material would be a sensible first buy.

A final note on an item of equipment which is easily forgotten: entrants to quiz walks or kanters should remember to carry a pencil or ballpoint pen and possibly a highlighter pen to mark tally cards or trace routes on OS maps.

Food and drink

It is important to eat well and sensibly both before and during an event, particularly on the longer, overnight walks. The quantity and quality of the food available vary enormously from event to event. Some day events offer only drinks (usually orange or lemon squash and water; sometimes tea and/or coffee), whilst other provide considerable quantities of food.

Events take place in all weather conditions. Here walkers are leaving Grassington at the start of the Trollers Trot

Favourites among challenge walkers include fruit cake, cold rice pudding, tinned fruit, jam and Marmite sandwiches, and a variety of biscuits. Whilst not perhaps forming the ideal daily diet under normal circumstances, these foodstuffs are high in carbohydrate and are easily eaten and digested when tired. They are ideal from the organisers' point of view, being easily purchased, transported to checkpoints and prepared, often under difficult circumstances.

However, it is never advisable to rely solely on food provided at an event. The quantity may be insufficient for your needs, or the type may not be to your liking. Furthermore, the logistics of feeding hundreds of walkers at a number of checkpoints are often complex and sometimes break down, resulting in walkers having to forego food at some checkpoints. The walker should not blame the organisers or helpers if this happens (it is, in fact, quite rare) and he or she has no provisions, but should consider it to be his or her own fault for not preparing for this eventuality.

When walking in the countryside spare food and drink should always be carried in case of emergency and this rule applies as much to the organised event as to an ordinary day walk on the hills. The nature of the food will obviously be a personal choice, but it is a good idea to carry easily digestible, energy-giving foodstuffs. Take your favourite foods, as these can be more easily eaten when you are tired and may help to raise jaded spirits during a 'low point' on the walk.

Always ensure that you drink enough whilst on an event. It is all too easy to become dehydrated, particularly on a very hot, sunny day. Drink plenty before you begin to feel intensely thirsty; if you leave it until this stage, then it may already be too late. Dehydration can lead to heat stroke and collapse if not treated as soon as possible. Some walkers prefer to drink one of the specialised isotonic drinks which replace important minerals lost during physical activity; these drinks can be purchased from good sports shops.

Time for refreshment at a checkpoint on the Cotswold Challenge.

On overnight events one or more substantial meals are usually provided at certain well-placed checkpoints or feeding stations along the way. The most significant meal on a Hundred event is the so-called 'breakfast stop' which is normally situated between half and two-thirds of the way along the route. It is designed in such a way that the majority of participants arrive some time during the morning of the second day. On longer events most organisers arrange for a variety of different foods to be available at the various checkpoints to cater for the likes and dislikes of participants and to provide a varied diet en route.

To sum up: the general rule is to eat 'little and often', so replacing lost calories without producing lethargy. It is becoming increasingly common for event organisers to provide a cooked meal at the walk headquarters at the end of the event; the price is often included in the entry fee (vegetarian meals are often available). Many challenge walkers enjoy this meal at the end of the walk before the journey home. It also adds to the social nature of the event.

On the walk

Checkpoints

The course of all challenge walk events and some anytime challenge walks is sub-divided into sections which end at a checkpoint (often abbreviated to CP). The number of checkpoints varies considerably depending on the decisions of the organisers and the needs of the particular event. They can be either manned or unmanned.

Manned checkpoints

Manned checkpoints serve three main functions.

1. They are points at which walkers can be identified and their progress along the course monitored. This is an especially important safety factor; if the walker becomes lost or injured it will be known when and where he or she was last seen.

2. Checkpoints are sometimes placed to ensure that every walker follows the full route without taking short-cuts. A participant who fails to report at every checkpoint in the correct sequence will be disqualified from the event.

3. They usually double-up as feeding stations.

On arrival at a checkpoint, hand in your walk card to the marshal on duty, but be sure to retrieve it before you continue on the route. Check that the tally has been punched correctly and give your walk number to the marshal, if required. Checkpoint staff are frequently overworked for certain periods when the majority of the walkers on the event arrive over a short space of time and consequently queues may build up. Please be patient.

Manned checkpoints usually have both opening and closing times. The opening times will usually be such that even the fastest walker should not arrive before the checkpoint is open. The closing times are calculated to allow the slowest walkers to reach the checkpoint in time, provided their pace is sufficient to enable them to finish the entire route within the allotted time. Where runners are allowed on the event or where staggered start times are in operation, the checkpoint opening and closing times will be varied accordingly. If you are asked to retire by the checkpoint marshals because you are 'out of time', then do so gracefully and try again next time.

Unmanned checkpoints

Unmanned checkpoints on challenge events are normally included in the course to ensure that walkers don't take short-cuts. They usually possess an orienteering-type punch which is used to pierce the tally in the appropriate position. Occasionally, they consist of a number or letter which must be written on the walk card as proof that the walker has visited the checkpoint.

It is sometimes necessary to answer a simple question at unmanned checkpoints on anytime challenge walks, e.g. the number of an OS trig. point or the name of a church. The list of answers is then sent to the walk recorder as proof that the walker has completed the route. A similar system often operates on kanters.

A checkpoint on the Clent Clamber in the West Midlands ▶

Navigation

It is surprising how many walkers, whether on challenge walks or on some other form of walking activity, have little or no knowledge of the use of map and compass. Anyone who explores the countryside on foot should give high priority to the understanding and practice of their use. Many publications are available which explain the rudiments of navigation and these should be studied at the earliest opportunity. The chapter on navigation in *Mountaincraft and Leadership* is particularly recommended (*see* 'Publications'). Further advice and assistance can be gained from fellow walkers.

The competent use of map and compass in the mountains and featureless moorland areas of Britain is absolutely vital. Practise whenever the opportunity arises, not only when thick cloud descends and visibility is severely limited. Quite simply, the ability to use map and compass may one day save your life. (The best sort of compass to buy is a Silva-type model, with baseplate and 'direction of travel' arrow.)

Route descriptions

For some events the ability to use map and compass is essential, as the walker must navigate between a number of given map grid references. It is more common, however, for a route description to be supplied, although the quality, reliability and detail of these can vary enormously. The organisers should not always be blamed for poor route descriptions, as it is a very difficult task to write a clear, entirely unambiguous description of a cross-country walk. Furthermore, things sometimes change quite rapidly in the countryside; a fence can be painted a different colour or a stile damaged or a footpath sign removed in the time between the route being 'walked out' and the day of the event. For this reason it is a good idea to follow the route on a map at the same time as the route description. In this way, if the line of the route is temporarily mislaid, the walker will know his or her position on the map. If walking with

a companion on an event, it is often convenient if one walker reads the route description whilst the other follows the route on the map.

All too often on challenge events walkers tend to follow the person in front without bothering to read their own route descriptions or maps. All is well until the person who actually knows the correct way disappears from sight. Those who have not been following the route carefully are then completely unaware of their position. Resist the temptation to follow the person in front; don't assume that those ahead know the route.

If the correct line is mislaid, be sure to follow public rights of way until the bona fide route is re-joined. Do not trespass; if you are caught by a landowner, the organiser will be blamed and this will put the future of the event in jeopardy.

Country code

Ensure that you read the Country Code and *always* obey it when in the countryside.

Enjoy the countryside and respect its life and work.
Guard against all risk of fire.
Fasten all gates.
Keep your dogs under close control.
Keep to public paths across farmland.
Use gates and stiles to cross fences, hedges and walls.
Leave livestock, crops and machinery alone.
Take your litter home.
Help to keep all water clean.
Protect wildlife, plants and trees.
Take special care on country roads.
Make no unnecessary noise.

Footpath erosion

The challenge walker has other responsibilities which should concern all those who love and care for the countryside. Erosion of footpaths in certain areas is a serious problem. So, don't patronise any event which crosses land known to be suffering from serious erosion and where damage is likely to be exacerbated by the tramping of large numbers of walkers. Other areas have the opposite problem: rights of way are obstructed and footpaths are not clearly visible.

The passage of a hundred or more walkers on such paths will do wonders in keeping them open. Support events which are organised in the less well frequented areas of the country.

However, remember that many people appreciate the tranquillity of the countryside as an escape from the rush and crowds of the cities. Think carefully before entering events that cater for thousands of participants; ask yourself if the countryside is the right place for such mass activities. Certainly, don't participate in any mass event which is organised over ecologically sensitive areas. If you feel strongly about such matters, then write to the organisers, stating your opinions.

Health and injuries

It is extremely unwise and foolhardy to take part in a challenge walk if you are suffering from a severe cold, influenza, sickness or diarrhoea. Long distance walking demands stamina and endurance which will not be forthcoming if the body is fighting an infection. Even a relatively simple ailment, such as a common cold, can easily develop into something far more serious if the sufferer walks for miles over cold and damp moorland.

Be sensible: there is always another occasion. Don't expect too much sympathy from the organisers of an event if you selfishly attempt the walk whilst ill; they will have to get medical or other assistance if you develop serious problems en route.

Although long distance walking is suitable for men and women of all ages, if you are over 60 and have never walked for more than a few miles in your life before, or if you have suspected heart or lung complaints, it is advisable to seek the advice of a doctor before taking up challenge walking.

Fortunately, injuries on walking events are not very common, but they do occur. Twisted or broken ankles are probably the most common result of a slip or fall, and broken legs and arms are inevitable from time to time when large numbers of walkers are taking to the countryside every weekend of the year. Far more common with long distance walkers are the 'over-use' injuries, particularly those associated with the knee, hip and ankle. An inappropriate type of footwear or incorrect gait are usual causes, and the only real way to deal with these injuries is to retire from the event and rest until they subside. To continue a walk under increasing amounts of pain is mere stupidity, and it could lead to more serious and longer-lasting injuries.

Blisters

Perhaps the most common minor injury to befall the walker is the foot blister. Those who have suffered bad blistering would probably disagree that this affliction could be classified a minor one: blisters can be excruciatingly painful. They are likely to occur on inexperienced walkers who have soft skin on their feet and who are unused to long hours walking on a variety of surfaces. The skin on the underpart of the foot tends to harden with frequent walking, after which the likelihood of blistering decreases.

Those prone to blistering should pay particular attention to footwear: a good fit is essential. High quality socks which fit well and do not move their position within the boot or trainer are advisable. Some walkers recommend wearing two pairs of socks, whilst others advocate putting vaseline on the feet to reduce the risk of blistering. Some people even resort to using surgical spirit to harden the feet.

As a final word of caution on blisters, be most careful if attempts are made to burst them to release the fluid and so ease the discomfort. This can often lead to infection and blood poisoning. If you decide to burst a blister, make sure that conditions are as sterile as possible. It is best to ask the advice beforehand of medical helpers who will normally be at hand on walking events.

Stiffness

It is not unusual to suffer some degree of 'stiffness' after a long distance walk. The extent of the problem is an indication of the individual's fitness. To combat stiffness, some walkers advocate a selection of simple 'warm down' exercises similar to those practised by runners. However, frequent exercise, coupled with adequate rest after long walks, are probably the best ways of coping with this problem.

Hypothermia

Hypothermia is a major cause of death in hillwalking accidents. You should study the causes, symptoms, recognition, avoidance and treatment before undertaking any arduous walking activity, particularly during the winter months, on walks into hill and moorland country, and on overnight events. The chapter on mountain hypothermia in *Mountaincraft and Leadership* (see 'Publications') is highly recommended. Heat exhaustion can also be a problem if you don't drink enough fluid during a strenuous walk on a hot day; this can have disastrous consequences.

Training

Walkers or ramblers who regularly walk up to 15 or more miles (24 km) in a day should require little preparation for one of the shorter events of between 20 and 25 miles (32 and 40 km) in length. It is true to say that the best preparation for walking is walking. After completing several of the shorter events, the challenge walker may wish to increase his or her mileage, eventually taking part in some of the longer, overnight events.

Many people need some form of exercise between events to maintain fitness. Some jog regularly; others keep fit by simply walking to and from work every day. Many take part in other types of walking activity, such as hill walking, backpacking or walking long distance trails, between challenges. The main aim is enjoyment; health and fitness are an added bonus.

Those who have never walked for more than a mile or two before would be advised to start slowly, with fairly low mileage. Several events have short distance options, sometimes as low as 6 miles (9.7 km). Try entering one or two of these shorter routes until this distance presents no problems, before gradually increasing the mileage.

This sort of advice may seem obvious, but so often newcomers to long distance walking attempt to walk too far, too soon, and so develop awful blisters and stiffness. The end result, of course, is that they are discouraged from further long distance walking.

Anytime challenges

Many people enjoy a long, hard walk in the countryside, but prefer to go alone or with a small group of friends rather than with many people on an organised event. Others would like to take up challenge walking, but circumstances prevent them from going to organised events. Such walkers may derive enjoyment and satisfaction from 'anytime' challenge walks. Many people, of course, enjoy both organised events and anytime challenge walks.

An anytime challenge walk can be tackled, as the name suggests, whenever the walker has time available. Most are circular and are ideally suited for day walks, making use of a private car to get to and from the start/finish point.

Most anytime challenges (*see* page 38) have an official recorder to whom brief details of the walk are sent and who will usually, for a small fee, issue a completion certificate/badge. See *Strider* and *Long Distance Walker's Handbook* for more details on anytime challenges.

Long distance paths and trails

Britain is fortunate in possessing several hundred long distance paths (LDPs) ranging in length from a mere 10 miles (16 km) to almost 600 miles (965 km). In addition to the well known National Trails (e.g. Pennine Way, South Downs Way, Ridgeway) there are many other LDPs that have been developed and waymarked by various County Councils (e.g. the 140-mile (225-km) Saxon Shore Way in Kent), the Ramblers' Association and its local groups (e.g. the 100-mile (160-km) Cotswold Way), many other walking clubs and organisations, and even individuals. With the support of the LDWA, Keith Chesterton has pioneered one such LDP, the London Countryway, which circumnavigates the capital for a distance of 205 miles (330 km). Details of over 340 paths, including all the major LDPs in Britain, will be found in the *Long Distance Walker's Handbook* (*see* 'Publications'). Another useful book is *Long Distance Paths: South-East England*.

Organisations

Challenge walking events are staged by a number of different national organisations and their various local groups and clubs. The two major organisations involved are the Long Distance Walkers Association, and the British Walking Federation.

Both the LDWA and the BWF offer an extensive calendar of events throughout the year, covering most areas of the country. The style of BWF and LDWA events is a little different. The BWF does not generally stage events which exceed 27 miles (43 km); in fact, there is usually a range of distances on offer, with the shortest distance sometimes as low as 6 miles (10 km). Many, but not all, BWF routes tend to be on tracks, minor roads or well defined footpaths, the trail usually being waymarked with temporary signs or stickers.

LDWA events are between 20 and 100 miles (32 and 160 km) in length, although several organisers also offer a shorter route to run concurrently with the principal event. A route description is often supplied on LDWA events, but the route is rarely waymarked, except occasionally over exceptionally difficult sections. Walking is mainly on footpaths or over open access land, road walking being kept to a minimum.

Long Distance Walkers Association

The aim of the Long Distance Walkers Association is to further the interests of those who enjoy long distance walking. Founded in 1972 by the late Alan Blatchford and by Christopher Steer, both from Surrey, the association now has a national membership in excess of 6,000 individuals.

Membership

Membership is open to all. There are three categories of membership: individual, family and affiliate (the latter is for clubs, schools and other groups).

Members of the LDWA have a common interest in walking long and ultra-long distances in rural, mountainous or moorland areas. There is little interest in road walking. The association promotes and organises challenge walking events and anytime challenge walks, pioneers new walking routes and long distance footpaths, and publishes information on all aspects of noncompetitive walking. It is recognised by the Sports Council as the governing body for long distance walking, and is

concerned with improving standards of organisation and participation.

Strider

The LDWA produces *Strider*, a magazine which is distributed to members three times a year in April, August and December. It consists of contributions from members and contains no advertisements. Each issue has approximately 100 pages and contains news of long distance paths, a comprehensive calendar of future events, reports of past events, full length articles on various aspects of long distance walking, book reviews, letters and features on the environment.

Local groups

Another of the benefits of membership is the opportunity to join a local group of the association, of which there are some 38 throughout England, Wales and Scotland. Each organises social walks, usually once a month, as well as other social and walking activities.

The walks and social programmes of all the groups appear in each issue of *Strider*, but most groups also keep their members informed by means of a regular newsletter. Many organise at least one challenge walking event every year. They travel to events together and pool transport, thereby cutting down costs and helping those without private transport.

The LDWA caters for many kinds of walking, from highly organised challenges to the most informal strolls. It is not concerned with race walking, or sponsored and charity walks, although many members do participate in these types of event. It also does not support any event that has more than 500 participants.

Further details of the LDWA, together with membership application forms, can be obtained by sending an SAE to the membership secretary (*see* 'Useful addresses'). Members benefit from a reduced entry fee at many challenge walking events and a number of retail outlets are willing to give discounts.

British Walking Federation

The British Walking Federation is a member of the international organisa-

tion known as the IVV (Internationaler Volkssportverband or the International Federation of Popular Sports). This was founded in 1968 to promote walking, cycling, swimming and skiing. The founding countries were Germany, Switzerland, Austria and Liechtenstein, but today several other European countries as well as the USA and Canada are members of IVV.

The Great Britain IVV was founded in 1983, but in 1989 it changed its name to the British Walking Federation, because walking had proved to be by far the most popular of the four sports. It is essentially a group of walking clubs committed to IVV principles and activities. Around 80 walking clubs throughout Britain have become members.

Awards

The IVV operates a scheme for rewarding its participants for their achievements. To join the scheme it is necessary to obtain, for a small fee, an official IVV log book in which to record events and distances covered. These are on sale at all BWF events.

The scheme enables participants to amass credits for taking part in walks registered with the BWF or any other member country's events. Credits can be gained for participation and for the distance completed.

Awards are first issued on the completion of 10 events or 310 miles (500 km) and are obtained by submitting completed log books to a national awards officer. There is no time limit on the redemption of awards. Award winners, who receive a special patch, stick-pin and certificate, appear in the 'hall of fame' sections of the BWF magazine *Footprint*.

Details of BWF (IVV) events will be found in the annual calendar of UK walks/marches, published by the BWF for each calendar year. Further information can be obtained by writing to the National Office (*see* 'Useful addresses').

A variety of disparate organisations stage challenge events. These include local groups of the Youth Hostels Association (YHA), local Scout troops, local groups of the Ramblers' Association (RA) and other walking clubs, mountain rescue teams, Police units and Fire services, the Samaritans, Christian Aid and the St John's Ambulance Brigade.

Useful addresses

Please enclose an SAE when writing for information.

Long Distance Walkers Association (LDWA) Membership Secretary, 7 Ford Drive, Yarnfield, Stone, Staffordshire ST15 0RP

British Walking Federation (IVV) National Office, P.O. Box 63, Bracknell, Berkshire RG12 4EW

Ramblers' Association (RA) 1/5 Wandsworth Road, London SW8 2XX Tel: (071) 582 6879

Youth Hostels Association (England and Wales) YHA, Trevelyan House, 8 St Stephens Hill, St Albans, Hertfordshire AL1 2DY Tel: (0727)55215

Anytime/Anywhere Group of the LDWA Secretary, 2 Sandy Lane, Beeston, Nottingham NG9 3GS

P & R Publicity (Achievement Badges) Queensway, Stem Lane, New Milton, Hampshire BH25 5NN Tel: (0425) 611911

Publications

Footprint – the official magazine of the BWF (IVV). Published four times a year.

The annual Calendar of UK Walks/Marches. Published by the BWF (IVV).

Guidelines for Events – published by the LDWA. Essential information for those considering organising a challenge walking event.

Long Distance Paths: South-East England by Alan Castle. Published 1990 by A & C Black.

Long Distance Walker's Handbook by B. Blatchford and J. Margetts with Sue Ramsey (4th Edition, 1990). Published by A & C Black.

Mountaincraft and Leadership by Eric Langmuir (1984). Published jointly by the Sports Council and Mountainwalking Leader Training Board.

Strider – magazine of the LDWA. Published in April, August and December. Available to members only.

Day events (table 1)

Name of event	Distance miles	km	Time limit (hrs)	Location	Time of year
South-East England					
Surrey Inns Kanter	13/20	21/32	$7\frac{1}{4}$	Surrey	January
Punchbowl	14/33	22/53	12	Surrey	February
Chanctonbury Marathon	9/15/26	14/24/42	9	South Downs	February
Sevenoaks Circular	30	48	10	Kent	March
Hertford Hobble	12/25	19/40	$9\frac{1}{2}$	Hertfordshire	July
Tanners Marathon	30	48	10	Surrey	July
Andredsweald Circuit	25	40	9	Kent/Sussex	July (Biennial)
Rother Valley Eagles Walk	8/17/25	13/27/40	–	South Downs	August
Tunbridge Wells Circular	13/18/25	21/29/40	–	Kent	August
Chiltern Marathon	27/33	43/53	$9–10\frac{1}{2}$	Buckinghamshire	September
Canterbury Circular	15/25/30	24/40/48	–	Kent	September
Meridian Walk	25	40	–	London, Essex, Hertfordshire	September
Blackwater Marathon	15/25	24/40	10	Essex	November (Biennial)
Gatliff Marathon	31	50	10	Kent/Sussex	December
Southern & South-West England					
Stonehenge Stomp	6/12/19/25	10/19/30/40	8	Wiltshire	January
New Forest Marathon	25	40	9	Hampshire	February
Amesbury Carnival Walk	6/12/19/25	10/19/30/40	$8\frac{1}{2}$	Wiltshire	May
Purbeck Plod	25	40	–	Dorset	June
Dorset Doddle	30	48	–	Dorset	August
Cotswold Challenge	25	40	10	Gloucestershire	September/October
Vectis 50K Walk	31	50	10	Isle of Wight	October
Sidmouth Saunter	25	40	10	Devon	October

Name of event	Distance miles	km	Time limit (hrs)	Location	Time of year
Midlands & East Anglia					
South Shropshire Circular	28	45	10	Shropshire	February
Daffodil Dawdle	27	43	12	Cambridgeshire	March
Nene Valley Kanter	15/26	24/42	9½	Northamptonshire	April
Leek Moors Marathon	30	48	12	Peak District	May
Boscobel Walk	9/16/25	14/26/40	–	Staffordshire/Shropshire	May
Six Shropshire Summits	36	58	–	Shropshire	June
Poppy Line Marathon	26	42	10	Norfolk	June
Malvern Marathon	35	56	13	Hereford & Worcester	June
Windmills & Watertowers	9/18/26	14/29/42	10	Cambridgeshire	September
Shotley Peninsula Challenge	15/25/30	24/40/48	–	Suffolk	September (Biennial)
Clent Clamber	17/26	27/42	–	West Midlands	September
Spires & Squires Marathon	15/25	24/40	10	Northamptonshire	October
Wales					
Reservoir Roundabout	25	35	–	Powys	January
Lord Crawshaw Memorial Walk	10/15/25	16/24/40	–	Powys	February
Mid-Wales Mountain Marathon	24	38	–	Gwynedd	April
Black Mountains Roundabout	25	40	10	Powys	April
Snowdonia Panoramic Walk	30	48	15	Gwynedd	June
Drovers Walk	10/15/25	16/24/40	12	Powys	June
Talybont Trial	20	32	–	Powys	September
Mystery Mountain Marathon	25	40	–	Gwent/Powys	September
Northern England					
Scarborough Rock Challenge	26	42	10½	North Yorkshire	January
Wheeldale Tandem	26	42	11	North York Moors	January

Name of event	Distance miles	km	Time limit (hrs)	Location	Time of year
Two Crosses Circuit	25	40	9	Lancashire	January
That's Lyth	20/28	32/45	–	Cumbria	January
Cleveland Survival	26	42	12	North York Moors	March
Blubberhouses Moor 25	25	40	10	North Yorkshire	April
Round of the Four Passes	18	29	10	Lake District	April
Spring in Lakeland	28	45	–	Lake District	May
Pendle Marathon	25	40	–	Lancashire	May
Saltergate Circuit	26	42	–	North Yorkshire	May
Ulfkil Stride	24/33	38/53	11	Yorkshire Dales	June
Silvarn Round	25	40	–	Various	June
Gongoozler	18/35	29/56	–	Various	June
Durham Dales Challenge	28	45	12	County Durham	July
Great Shunner Shuffle	29	46	11	Yorkshire Dales	July
Anglezarke Amble	21	34	–	Lancashire	July & February
Limestone Limp	38	61	12	Yorkshire Dales	August
Smugglers Trod	26	42	11	North York Moors	August
Cheviots Challenge Walk	26	42	12	Northumberland	August
Wigan Pier Walk	15/27	24/43	–	Lancashire	September
Falcon Flyer	26	42	12	North York Moors	October
Wide Awake Walk	23	37	–	Forest of Bowland	October
Hallowe'en Happening	30	48	–	Lancashire	October
Kilburn Kanter	28	45	10	North Yorkshire	November

Scotland

Name of event	Distance miles	km	Time limit (hrs)	Location	Time of year
Pentlands Marathon	26	42	12	Lothian	June
Three Lochs Challenge	24/10	39/16	–	Highland	June

Multi-day events (table 2)

Name of event	Number of days	Distance miles	km	Location	Organiser	Time of year
Aylesbury Amble	2	2 × 25 2 × 12 2 × 6	2 × 40 2 × 19 2 × 10	Chilterns	Aylesbury Amblers	April
Across Ross Walk	2	60	96	Scottish Highlands	LDWA Scots members	May
Ultimate Challenge	up to 16	Own route coast to coast across Scotland		Scottish Highlands	*The Great Outdoors* magazine	May
Tanners Two-Day Walk	2	2 × 20/30 2 × 10	2 × 32/48 2 × 16	Surrey	Tanners Hatch YH	July
York International 4-Day Walks	4	4 × 25 4 × 15 4 × 9	4 × 40 4 × 24 4 × 14	North Yorks	North London Walkers & Road Marching Association	August
Welsh International 4-Day Walks	4	4 × 20/25 4 × 15 4 × 10	4 × 32/40 4 × 24 4 × 16	Mid-Wales	BWF(IVV)	September
Real Ale Amble	2	2 × 25 2 × 10 2 × 6	2 × 40 2 × 16 2 × 10	Mid-Wales	—	November

Ultra-long distance (overnight) events (table 3)

Name of event	Distance miles	km	Time Limit (hrs)	Location	Organiser	Time of year
Sheriffs Way	52	83	24	Nottinghamshire	Scouts	February
High Peak Marathon	40	64	–	Peak District	Sheffield University YH Society	March
Surrey Summits	62.5	100	26.5	Central & western Surrey	LDWA	March–April
Fellsman Hike	60	96	–	North Yorks	Scouts	May
80 miles South Downs Way	80	129	27	Sussex	Fellbridge Juniors Rugby Club	June
Lakes Four Three Thousand Peaks Trial	46	74	22	Lake District	RA	June
South Wales Marathon Walk	47	75	–	Dyfed/Powys	YHA	June
North York Moors Crosses Walk	54	86	24	North Yorks	Scarborough & District Search & Rescue Team	July
Across Wales Walk*	45	72	18	Powys/Dyfed	YHA	September
Bullock Smithy Hike	56	90	24	Peak District	Scouts	September
Cleveland Classic	56	90	24	North York Moors	Camphill Village Trust	September
Anglian Heights Challenge	62.5	100	28	Cambs/Herts	LDWA	October
Longmynd Hike	50	80	24	Shropshire	Scouts	October
Wealden Waters Walk	62.5	100	26	Kent/Sussex	LDWA	October
Three Forests Way	60	96	28	Essex	LDWA	November

*Not an overnight walk

Anytime challenge walks (table 4)

Name of walk	Distance miles	km	Location
Ainsty Bounds	44	70	North Yorkshire
Amberley Amble	20	32	Bewdley, Worcestershire
Bell Walk Major	36	58	Peak District
Bilsdale Circuit	30	48	East Yorkshire
Brontë Round	23	37	Western Pennines
Carpet Baggers 50	50	80	Worcestershire & Staffordshire
Churnet Valley Challenge Walk	24	38	Staffordshire
Cloud 7 Circuit	33	53	North Staffordshire & Cheshire
Dales Traverse	25	40	Yorkshire Dales
Downland Church Walk	38	61	South Downs, West Sussex
Duddon Landscape	23	37	Lake District
East Thriding Treble Ten	30	48	East Yorkshire Wolds
Furness Five Trigs	19	30	Cumbria
Helm Wind Walk	20	32	Northern Pennines
High Street Stroll	30	48	Lake District
John Merrill's Dales Walk	25	40	Yorkshire Dales
John Merrill's NYM Challenge	24	38	North York Moors
John Merrill's Peak Challenge	25	40	Peak District
Kinver Clamber	20	32	Worcestershire
Langbaurgh Loop	38	61	North York Moors
Mini-Alps	20	32	Malverns, Worcestershire
Nidd Vale Circuit	26	42	Yorkshire Dales
North to South Surrey Walk	39	62	Surrey

Ramblers Way	38	61	Peak District
Rosedale Circuit	37	59	North York Moors
Shepherds Round	40	64	North York Moors
Shieldsman	36	58	Tyneside
Spanners Round	20	32	Western Pennines
Surrey Hills Walk	50	80	Surrey
Three Feathers – 1st Feather	30	48	Yorkshire Dales
2nd Feather	30	48	North York Moors
3rd Feather	26	42	Peak District
Three Reservoirs Challenge	25	40	Peak District
Wyre Forest Alpine Walk	20	32	Worcestershire

*The Flamborough Fling Spring Challenge is a
26-mile walk within 10 hours – over the
Yorkshire Wolds and Heritage Coast –
organised by the Bridlington Boys Club*

◀ *Long distance walkers in Painswick on the
Cotswolds Way*

Doing all the paperwork. Marshals on the Brecon Beacons Hundred review registration details in order to check how many entrants have started the event

Badge and certificate designs for two anytime challenge walks. Top, the Wyre Forest Alpine Walk (20 miles/32km) in the West Midlands. Bottom, the 22-mile (35km) Chaddesley Chase, starting from the Worcestershire village of Chaddesley Corbett ▶

Appendix

Clothing and Equipment

The list below gives typical clothing and equipment requirements for entrants to challenge walks. This list does not cover hill/mountain walking requirements in winter; neither is it a definitive list of requirements. It may be useful as a helpful check-list.

adequate footwear
rucksack
waterproof top and overtrousers
drink (hot/cold) and mug
emergency food, e.g. chocolate bars
compass
map(s) and map case
route description
torch, spare batteries and bulb
extra sweater
first-aid kit
white/luminous/reflective patches for
    night walking
telephone money
survival bag
whistle
spare laces